YOUR KNOWLEDGE HAS VALUE

- We will publish your bachelor's and master's thesis, essays and papers

- Your own eBook and book - sold worldwide in all relevant shops

- Earn money with each sale

Upload your text at www.GRIN.com and publish for free

A survey of Machine Learning Models for Prediabetes Screening

Amos Olwendo

Bibliographic information published by the German National Library:

The German National Library lists this publication in the National Bibliography; detailed bibliographic data are available on the Internet at http://dnb.dnb.de.

ISBN: 9783389117255
This book is also available as an ebook.

© GRIN Publishing GmbH
Trappentreustraße 1
80339 München

All rights reserved

Print and binding: Books on Demand GmbH, Norderstedt, Germany
Printed on acid-free paper from responsible sources.

The present work has been carefully prepared. Nevertheless, authors and publishers do not incur liability for the correctness of information, notes, links and advice as well as any printing errors.

GRIN web shop: https://www.grin.com/document/1567635

A survey of Machine Learning Models for Prediabetes Screening

Background and Purpose: Diabetes is gradually becoming a global challenge owing to the gradual increase in the number of cases of Type 2 diabetes mellitus (T2DM). T2DM is characterized as a state of hyperglycaemia due to abnormal control of insulin levels that eventually affects metabolism. This study aimed to review articles that implement machine learning methods to identify suitable risk factors for prediabetes.

Methods: The study adopted the preferred reporting items for systematic review (PRISMA) protocol and research questions were formulated by the identification of synonyms and related terms "predictors and prediabetes and machine learning" from PubMed and Google scholar. Both observational and interventional original articles that were published between 2018 and 2023 were included in this study. Eligibility for inclusion was determined by scanning the article title, abstract, and study methodology section.

Results: Four articles focusing on prediabetes conducted in Hong-Kong, rural India, Korea, and USA were examined. Prediabetes was mainly defined using the American guidelines for the diagnosis of prediabetes. Machine learning algorithms examined for creation of the models include support vector machine, extreme gradient boosting, and random forest. Model performances were validated using the AUC-ROC and F1-Score.

Conclusions: Effective management of diabetes requires an early diagnosis of prediabetes whose prevalence affects the overall burden of the disease in a population. Articles examined in this review achieved good model performances. However, there is need to generalize prediabetes screening tools to the global community since the predictors are similar across racial and ethnic disparities.

Keywords: Prediabetes, Risk Prediction, Machine Learning, Decision Support Systems

1 Introduction

1.1   Situation of Diabetes Mellitus

Diabetes is 3rd leading cause of mortality globally with an increasing prevalence of Type 2 diabetes mellitus (T2DM). The World Health Organization (WHO) reported in June 2018 that non-communicable diseases are responsible for nearly 40 million deaths yearly and diabetes mellitus is responsible for about 1.6 million deaths globally. The global prevalence of diabetes was 9.3% in 2019 and nearly 85% of mortalities related to diabetes were recorded in developing countries. Moreover, the prevalence of diabetes in emerging economies is expected to be on the rise as a result of sedentary lifestyles and the consumption of processed foods. Therefore, diabetes is projected to be the next epidemic in low-income countries as a result of the changing lifestyles prompted by the consumption of unwholesome diets that involve the intake of high amounts of calories as a result of socioeconomic progress [1].

Sub-Saharan Africa (SSA) is reporting the fastest-growing rates of the number of cases of diabetes globally. Nearly 523,000 mortalities in SSA were due to diabetes in 2014, and 76% of them were below 60 years of age. Furthermore, by the year 2035, it is predicted that about 41 million people in the SSA will suffer from diabetes. Delayed diagnosis of Type 1 diabetes mellitus (T1DM) is a primary reason for developing life-threatening complications of T1DM such as ketoacidosis and heightened hypoglycaemia. However, insufficient information regarding the statistics of diabetes within the East African region remains an issue of concern. However, a family history of diabetes and a high level of education in the family are identified as protective factors against the development and progression of diabetes.

In Kenya, a number of cases of diabetes are diagnosed late, and the prevalence of diabetes among Kenyans aged between 20 and 79 years was approximated at 484,000 persons in 2015. A recent study by [1] reported the prevalence of T2DM (92%). Also, prediabetes, a state of a glycaemic level higher than 6.0 mm/L and lower than 7.0 mm/L remains a significant feature for the development of diabetes and its subsequent complications. Thus, knowledge of the prevalence of prediabetes is vital for accurate future projections of diabetes, especially T2DM. Studies conducted in the United States of America (USA) and China approximates the prevalence of prediabetes between 36 - 50% [2]. Earlier studies in Kenya estimated the prevalence of prediabetes to be within the range of 3% to 5%. However, the study by [3] conducted at Nairobi Hospital reported a prevalence for prediabetes at (0.4% and unidentified cases of diabetes (40%) (based on the International Classification of Diseases version 10 codes). Since cases of prediabetes are believed to progress into T2DM and the prevalence of T2DM was reported at 92%, then it's logical to believe all unidentified cases of diabetes were undiagnosed cases of prediabetes [4].

1.2 Introduction to Machine Learning

Machine learning is a discipline that deals with the use of data and algorithms to reproduce human actions. Machine learning is an important domain in the rising field of Data Science. With the application of statistical methods, computer algorithms learn to classify data and make appropriate predictions thus discovering important insights. Machine learning algorithms are categorized as; supervised, semi-supervised, and unsupervised learning methods. Supervised learning is defined by the use of labeled datasets to train the algorithms that it uses to forecast results. Input data, also known as the training data, are subjected to the model and it's upon the model to adjust the weights until the model appropriately fits the function. The general idea in supervised learning includes defining a learning function $y = f(x)$ from the inputs data x and their corresponding outcomes y. Thereafter, the algorithm is expected to predict the outcomes for the test dataset. Supervised learning is best applied for classification tasks such as disease diagnosis where the outcome is either present or absent. Common supervised methods include can be sub-categorized as regression, decision trees, Naïve Bayes, and support vector machine [3], [5].

On the other hand, unsupervised learning utilizes algorithms to analyze and group unlabelled datasets. These sets of algorithms determine patterns or groups in data. In unsupervised learning, the learning function determines essential features about the distribution of the inputs x and the outcomes y from the training dataset. Afterward, when the unsupervised trained model encounters a test dataset, it determines the outcome of every data record based on the previously learned function. The main unsupervised learning problems include association, clustering, and dimensionality reduction The capability of unsupervised learning algorithms to learn likenesses and variances in data makes these algorithms essential in exploratory data analysis and pattern recognition among other applications. Unsupervised learning methods are applied for the reduction of the number of features in a model using algorithms such as principal component analysis (PCA) and singular value decomposition (SVD). Other examples of unsupervised learning algorithms include fuzzy C-means, DBSCAN, k-means, and Mean –shift. Ensemble learning algorithms include; bagging, boosting, and stacking while reinforcement learning includes genetic algorithm [6].

2 Materials and methods

This systematic review adopted the PRISMA review protocol that helps research to source accurate information. The search for relevant literature began with the formulation of the research question. The search for literature began with the identification of synonyms and related terms ("predictors" and "prediabetes" and "machine learning") from PubMed and Google Scholar. The search for literature lasted two weeks (27th March 2023 to 2nd April 2023) and a total of 2450 articles were obtained. The inclusion criteria were; both observational and interventional journal articles written in English and published between 2018 and 2023. Studies such as systematic reviews, comments from editors, conference abstracts, and books were excluded. Eligibility for inclusion was focused on articles that focused on the study objectives and this was determined by scanning the study title and abstract. Through this process, a total of 55 articles were selected and through further filtering, 52 articles focused on statistical methods or articles focused on other types of diabetes or complications of diabetes were excluded from this analysis.

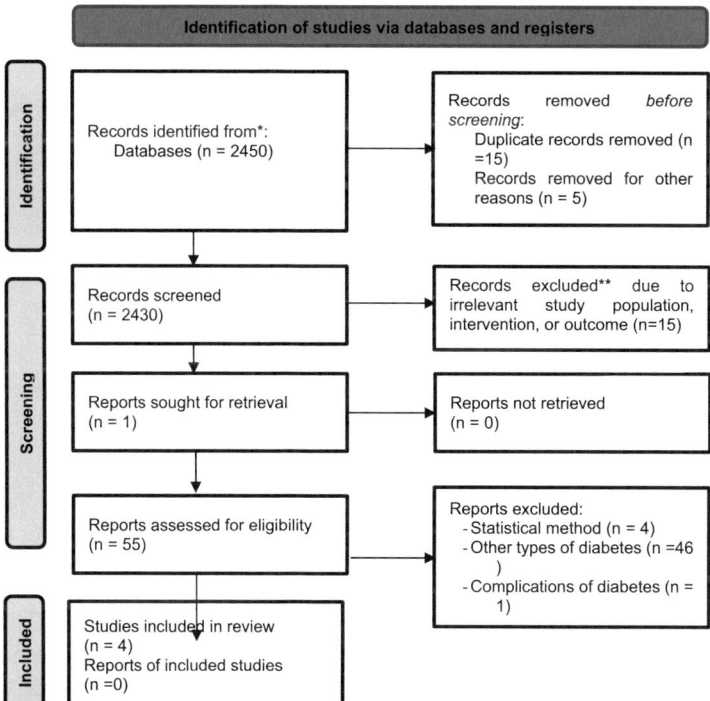

Figure 1: A summary of the systematic search strategy edited from PRASMA protocol [7].

2.1 Data Extraction and Analysis

1. W. Dong et al.

The problem the researchers/authors addressed. In this paper, the authors proposed a non-laboratory-based risk assessment model for case detection of diabetes mellitus and prediabetes using socio-demographic, lifestyle, and clinical parameters.

Previous work referred to by the authors. The authors referred to a number of risk assessment models for diabetes that have been developed and incorporated into diabetes prevention worldwide. These include American Center of Disease Control (CDC) prediabetes screening tool, and Leicester Self-Assessment score.

New ideas, algorithms. The authors added the need for assessment for sleep duration of 7 or 8 hours, consumption of vegetables and fruits, and vigorous physical activity time.

Experiments and analysis conducted. The authors conducted a rigorous statistical analysis for the risk factors. The differences of each risk factor among were compared using analysis of variance (ANOVA) for continuous variables and Chi-square for categorical variables. Post hoc pairwise comparison P values were adjusted by the Bonferroni method. Multicollinearity of the predictors was diagnosed using variance inflation factors (VIF) based on the full logistic regression model.

Results that the authors claim to have achieved. The authors claim their risk was validated using area under the receiver-operating characteristic curve (AUC-ROC) of 0.82 and precision-recall curve (AUC-PR) of 0.496.

Claims made by the authors. Sleep duration and rigorous recreational activity are modifiable risk factors for prediabetes and diabetes.

2. N. Birk et al.

The problem the researchers/authors addressed. In this paper, the authors used several machine learning techniques and compare their performances using AUC-ROC, for the development of a predictive model for prediabetes.

Previous work referred to by the authors. The authors do not refer to any to any previous work exactly on this topic.

New ideas, algorithms. Other than a rigorous analysis of participant's quality of diet using the Global Diet Quality Score (GDQS), the authors have not presented any new ideas or algorithms.

Experiments and analysis conducted. The analyses conducted a comparison of the performance of a number of statistical and machine learning models; random forest, generalized linear mixed model (GLMM), least absolute shrinkage and selection operator (LASSO).

Results that the authors claim to have achieved. The prevalence of prediabetes was 21% and the mean GDQS score for all participants 19.0 out of 42.5 points. The GLMM achieved an AUC-ROC of 0.77 and a sensitivity of 0.717.

Claims made by the authors. The authors believed that their success in this study indicated the possibility of developing a predictive tool for detection of cases of prediabetes.

3. K. De Silva et al.

The problem the researchers/authors addressed. In this paper, the authors purposed to identify predictors of prediabetes using feature selection and machine learning algorithms.

Previous work referred to by the authors. The authors referred to the CDC prediabetes tool that was used for the validation of their model.

New ideas, algorithms. The authors explored a number of predictors for prediabetes which include; socio-economic, clinical, and biochemical characteristics.

Experiments and analysis conducted. The authors conducted an analysis of the performances of algorithms; random forest, artificial neural network (ANN), logistic regression, and extreme gradient boosting (XGB)

Results that the authors claim to have achieved. The prevalence of prediabetes in the sampled dataset was 23.43% and the random forest and XGB algorithms attained AUC-ROC of 0.72 and 0.71 respectively.

Claims made by the authors. The combined use of feature selection and machine learning was useful in identifying a range of socio-economic, physiological, and biochemical predictors of prediabetes.

4. Yuk et al.

The problem the researchers/authors addressed. In this paper, the authors purposed to develop machine learning for the prediction of prediabetes.

Previous work referred to by the authors. The authors did not refer to any previous work exactly on this topic.

New ideas, algorithms. The authors explored a wide range of predictors (57) which included socio-demographic, clinical, and biochemical data.

Experiments and analysis conducted. The authors first conducted a chi-square test on the study variables for the selection of appropriate features. Thereafter, the authors conducted an analysis of the performances of algorithms; Logistic Regression, Naïve Bayes, Support Vector Machine, Random Forest, Extremely Randomized Tree, Extreme Gradient Boosting, Light Gradient Boosting Machine (Light GBM), and Multi-Layer Perceptron.

Results that the authors claim to have achieved. The Support Vector Machine (SVM), Light GBM, and the Multi-Layer Perceptron (MLP) algorithms attained AUC-ROC of 0.78 and F1 score of 0.45, 0.49, and 0.23 respectively.

Claims made by the authors. The SVM algorithm had the optimum performance; fasting blood glucose and HbA1c were the predominant predictors for prediabetes. Also, features related to the functioning of the liver; gamma-glutamyl transpeptidase can predict the development and progression of prediabetes.

3 Results

Four research articles with a goal on the creation of a predictive prototype for case finding for prediabetes that were published between 2019 and 2022. Two articles targeted specific population groups; Chinese in Hong Kong (1) and rural India (1), and two other models were meant for the general populations in North America and Korea respectively. All four articles had models made from socio-demographic/economic, clinical, and biochemical characteristics. However, upon selection of predictor for prediabetes, three articles listed relatively similar modifiable risk factors such as bodily activity, diet, smoking status, sleep duration, and use of alcoholic substances. Also, all four articles adopted the American Diabetes Association (ADA) guidelines for the diagnoses of prediabetes which is defined as fasting plasma glucose of 100–125 mg/dl, or HbA1c of 5.7–6.4%. The main machine learning algorithms used for model development include; random forest, extreme gradient boosting, and artificial neural network; multi-layer perceptron, support vector machine, and Light gradient boosting machine. The study conducted by W. Dong et al. used the extreme gradient boosting algorithm that posted the best results with an AUC-ROC of 0.82. The second best algorithm; light gradient boosting machine by H. Yuk et al. with an AUC-ROC of 0.78. The third best performing algorithm; GLMM by N. Birk et al. attained an AUC-ROC of 0.77. Finally, the study by K. De Silva et al. used the random forest algorithm that an AUC-ROC of 0.72. The other details are summarized in Table 1.

Table 1: Summary of research findings for machine learning prediction models for prediabetes.

Author	Sampling frame	Sample size	Risk factors	Prediabetes Definition	Machine Learning Algorithm	Outcome
W. Dong et al.	aged 18–84 years without self-reported diabetes mellitus, pre-diabetes mellitus, and other major chronic diseases	1857	- Age - BMI - WHR - Smoking status - Sleep duration - Vigorous recreational activity time per week - Fruit/vegetable consumption per week	Fasting plasma glucose of 100–125 mg/dl, oral glucose tolerance test of 140–200mg/dl, or HbA1c of 5.7–6.4%	Extreme Gradient Boosting was the only algorithm examined in this study	AUC-ROC = 0.82
N. Birk et al.	Age ≥18 years and had complete information on age, sex, blood glucose, select demographic information	5655	- Age, - Use of tobacco - Alcoholic consumption - Time spent in sedentary activities - Global Diet Quality Score	Fasting blood glucose measurement ≥100 mg/dL	- GLMM had optimal performance than other algorithms	AUC-ROC = 0.77
K. De Silva et al.	- Age 18–84 years - No prior diabetes - No prior prediabetes - No chronic diseases - No variables with 30% or more missing data were	6346	- Age - BMI - SBP - Waist circumference - Use of tobacco - Sleep duration - Physical activity	Fasting plasma glucose of 6.1–6.9 mmol/L or HbA1c of 5.7–6.4%	- Random forest performed better than the other algorithms	AUC-ROC = 0.72

9

| H. Yuk et al. | - Included records with attributes supported by a medical expert
- Excluded attributes with multicollinearity (to lower VIF<10)
- Excluded records with missing values > 20% | 22722 | - Age
- Body Fat Percentage
- BMI
- Waist circumference
- Force Vital Capacity
- Pulse Rate
- Hematocrit
- Alanine Transaminase
- Gamma-Glutamyl Transferase
- Triglycerides
- Fasting blood glucose
- HbA1c | - Fasting plasma glucose of 100–125 mg/dl | Light gradient boosting machine (Light GBM) performed better than all other algorithms examined. | AUC-ROC = 0.78 and F1 score = 0.49 |

4 Discussion

Prediabetes is increasingly becoming a worldwide health concern hence there is need for timely diagnosis of prediabetes within the routine healthcare setting. The first step in this endeavour requires identification of the most essential predictors for prediabetes. This process requires a thorough analysis of the many variables that have a role to play in the onset and progression of prediabetes. Furthermore, a predictive tool to be used in the primary healthcare setting should adhere to usability guidelines in addition to making such a device simple and easy to use. Therefore, during the process of identifying the predictors, it is essential to only focus on the factors that greatly contribute to the onset and progress of the disease. This requires correlation analysis [8], [9] and the use of dimensionality reduction algorithms such as PCA and SVD to only select the essential features in the dataset [10]. Furthermore, the process of feature selection may also employ the use of filtering, embedment, and wrapping algorithms such as SelectKBest, lasso, and Boruta. However, its important to understand that each of the feature selection algorithms is context-specific and there instances they can never be effective [11].

Also, it's essential to focus on predictors that are easily accessible. Essential risk factors for prediabetes can be categorized as; socio-demographic/economic, clinical, lifestyle, and family history. W. Dong et al. and N. Birk et al. focused on modifiable features. K. De Silva et al. model had modifiable and non-modifiable features that required laboratory examination. However, a good model should be simple and time efficient thus the use of features that require external examination may consume much time rendering such models less useful within the primary setting. Therefore, a good predictive tool will not only limit the number of predictors but also focus on risk factors that are readily available. Furthermore, for the case of screening and managing of prediabetes, a focus on the modifiable risk factors may be more beneficial than non-modifiable predictors [5], [12].

Three articles by [2], [8], [10] created models for screening for prediabetes using a limited choice of supervised machine learning methods yet there are many other supervised algorithms that could deliver stellar performances. For instance, K. De Silva et al. and N. Birk et al. compared supervised methods with basic regression and linear methods. However, these authors could have done better. De Silva and his colleagues compared XGB and random forest with an ANN model. However, details about the algorithm and the structure of the ANN model are not provided. Furthermore, unsupervised algorithms are best applied in exploratory data analysis and semi-supervised methods could be best applied in the event that there is not much-labeled dataset thus authors looking into developing predictive tools for prediabetes need to expand their choice of algorithms for model development [3], [6].

The task of validation of a prognostic archetype is very essential in confirming the results and also providing assurance for the repeatability of the given research. In this review, only Dong and his colleagues had an elaborate plan for the validation of their model. W. Dong et al. rigorously conducted correlational analysis for the predictors. Even though all the authors conducted a measure for the area under the curve (AUC-ROC) for the overall performance of the model using the test data set, W. Dong et al. went further to measure model sensitivity and recall. However, it's good practice that machine learning practitioners also measure the F1-score, precision, and recall for their models [13], [14].

In conclusion, few studies have been published on the prediction models for prediabetes since a number of articles have been generalized to diabetes. However, effective diabetes management requires an early diagnosis of prediabetes whose prevalence affects the overburden of diabetes within a given population. Even though the four articles examined in this review achieved modest performances, this examination highlights the fact that the heterogeneity of the study variables and methods may have provided results that can be generalized globally. Attempts to provide solutions to the need for early prediction of prediabetes need to be globalized thus machine learning practitioners should follow in the footsteps of the US CDC for the creation of a tool for screening for prediabetes that is applicable to people from all backgrounds. No matter a person's background or rather the reasons for the development and progress of prediabetes, the key characteristics of prediabetes remain similar irrespective of the patient's background. W. Dong et al, N. Birk et al. and N. De Silva et al. began their search for predictors for prediabetes with a rigorous examination of diet and biochemical features respectively. At the end of this process, all three articles ended up with a choice of predictors that are more or else similar. This confirms the need to generalize the measure for the likelihood for prediabetes with the help of machine learning algorism [6], [13].

Acknowledgements

I would like to acknowledge Madam Amina for support while working on this study.

Statement on conflicts of interest

There are no conflicts of interest with this work.

References

[1]   A. O. Olwendo, G. Ochieng, and K. Rucha, 'Prevalence and Complications Associated with Diabetes Mellitus at the Nairobi Hospital, Nairobi City County, Kenya', *J. Health Inform. Afr.*, vol. 7, no. 2, Art. no. 2, 2020, doi: 10.12856/JHIA-2020-v7-i2-290.

[2]   N. Birk *et al.*, 'Exploration of Machine Learning and Statistical Techniques in Development of a Low-Cost Screening Method Featuring the Global Diet Quality Score for Detecting Prediabetes in Rural India', *J. Nutr.*, vol. 151, no. Supplement_2, pp. 110S-118S, Oct. 2021, doi: 10.1093/jn/nxab281.

[3]   A. O. Olwendo, G. Ochieng, and K. Rucha, 'Suitability of Electronic Health Record Data for Computational Phenotyping of Diabetes Mellitus at Nairobi Hospital, Nairobi City County, Kenya | East African Journal of Science, Technology and Innovation', vol. 2, no. 2, Mar. 2021, doi: https://doi.org/10.37425/eajsti.v2i2.224.

[4]   F. Moradpour *et al.*, 'Prevalence of prediabetes, diabetes, diabetes awareness, treatment, and its socioeconomic inequality in west of Iran', *Sci. Rep.*, vol. 12, no. 1, Art. no. 1, Oct. 2022, doi: 10.1038/s41598-022-22779-9.

[5]   A. M. Nawi, P. S. N. M. Kamaruddin, N. R. M. Nordin, S. S. S. Soffian, and M. Baharom, 'Machine Learning Models in Prediabetes Screening: A Systematic Review', *J. Clin. Diagn. Res.*, vol. 16, no. 5, pp. 1–9, May 2022, doi: 10.7860/JCDR/2022/53411.16385.

[6]   A. Adler, 'Using Machine Learning Techniques to Identify Key Risk Factors for Diabetes and Undiagnosed Diabetes'. arXiv, May 19, 2021. doi: 10.48550/arXiv.2105.09379.

[7]   M. J. Page *et al.*, 'The PRISMA 2020 statement: an updated guideline for reporting systematic reviews', *BMJ*, vol. 372, p. n71, Mar. 2021, doi: 10.1136/bmj.n71.

[8]   W. Dong *et al.*, 'Non-laboratory-based risk assessment model for case detection of diabetes mellitus and pre-diabetes in primary care', *J. Diabetes Investig.*, vol. 13, no. 8, pp. 1374–1386, 2022, doi: 10.1111/jdi.13790.

[9]   W. Dong *et al.*, 'Development and validation of a diabetes mellitus and prediabetes risk prediction function for case finding in primary care in Hong Kong: a cross-sectional study and a prospective study protocol paper', *BMJ Open*, vol. 12, no. 5, p. e059430, May 2022, doi: 10.1136/bmjopen-2021-059430.

[10]   K. De Silva, D. Jönsson, and R. T. Demmer, 'A combined strategy of feature selection and machine learning to identify predictors of prediabetes', *J. Am. Med. Inform. Assoc.*, vol. 27, no. 3, pp. 396–406, Mar. 2020, doi: 10.1093/jamia/ocz204.

[11]   H. Yuk, J. Gim, J. K. Min, J. Yun, and T.-Y. Heo, 'Artificial Intelligence-based Prediction of Diabetes and Prediabetes Using Health Checkup Data in Korea', vol. 36, no. 1, p. 3772, Nov. 2022.

[12]   E. Buccheri, D. Dell'Aquila, and M. Russo, 'Artificial intelligence in health data analysis: The Darwinian evolution theory suggests an extremely simple and zero-cost large-scale screening tool for prediabetes and type 2 diabetes', *Diabetes Res. Clin. Pract.*, vol. 174, p. 108722, Apr. 2021, doi: 10.1016/j.diabres.2021.108722.

[13]   L. Shahmoradi, A. Otieno Olwendo, H. Arab-Alibeik, K. Agin, and S. Setareh, 'A Probabilistic Model for COPD Diagnosis and Phenotyping Using Bayesian Networks', *J. Community Health Res.*, vol. 6, no. 1, pp. 34–43, Feb. 2017.

[14]   A. Olwendo, L. Shahmoradi, and K. Agin, 'Probabilistic Model for Chronic Obstructive Pulmonary Disease Diagnosis and Phenotyping using Bayesian Network', in *Environment and Water Resource Management / 837: Health Informatics / 838: Modelling and Simulation / 839: Power and Energy Systems - 2016*, Gaborone, Botswana: ACTA Press, Sep. 2016. doi: 10.2316/P.2016.838-005.

YOUR KNOWLEDGE HAS VALUE

- We will publish your bachelor's and
  master's thesis, essays and papers

- Your own eBook and book -
  sold worldwide in all relevant shops

- Earn money with each sale

Upload your text at www.GRIN.com
and publish for free